This journal belongs to:

____

PENGUIN YOUNG READERS LICENSES
An imprint of Penguin Random House LLC
1745 Broadway, New York, NY 10019
penguinrandomhouse.com

Illustrations by Saskia Bueno

Design by Hsiao-Pin Lin

First published in the United States of America by
Penguin Young Readers Licenses, 2025

Manufactured in China
TOPL

ISBN 9798217052073
10 9 8 7 6 5 4 3 2 1

The authorized representative in the EU for product safety and compliance is Penguin Random House Ireland, Morrison Chambers, 32 Nassau Street, Dublin D02 YH68, Ireland, https://eu-contact.penguin.ie.

TIME for KIDS

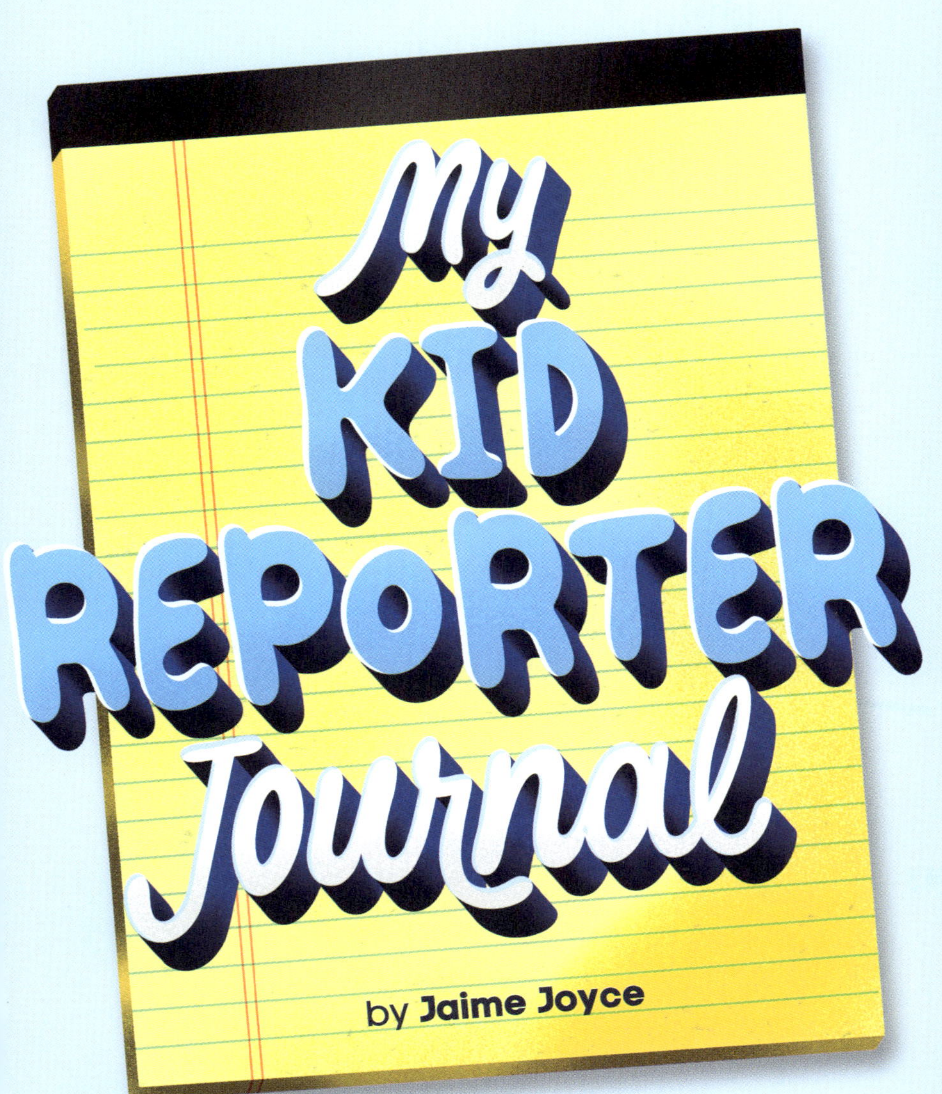

My Kid Reporter Journal

by Jaime Joyce

Welcome, young journalist! The book you hold in your hands contains 100 writing prompts that will get you in the habit of thinking like a true journalist. You'll brainstorm story ideas, come up with interview questions, and do the same kind of reporting and writing that professionals do on the job every day. Think of these writing prompts as exercises to build your journalistic muscles. With enough practice and consistent effort, you'll strengthen your skills and produce powerful work—and you'll be on the path to becoming a successful journalist!

To learn more about the exciting world of journalism, check out *TIME for Kids: Kid Reporter Field Guide*. It's the companion book to this trusty journal. You can also find reported stories online at timeforkids.com. Before using the internet to read stories or research topics, make sure you have the permission of your parent or guardian.

In this book, writing prompts are organized into six sections:

✦ JOURNALISM BASICS

Prompts in this section focus on the nuts and bolts of being a journalist, such as developing story ideas, taking notes, conducting interviews, and pitching (presenting your ideas) to an editor. These prompts will help you build a firm foundation for your journalistic work.

✦ NEWS COVERAGE

These prompts are all about covering current events. They're designed to train your attention on what's going on at school, in your community, across the country, and around the world so you can do accurate, fair, and fact-based reporting.

✦ OPINION WRITING

Opinion journalists share their point of view on current events. Their articles spark discussions and give readers the opportunity to consider perspectives that may be different from their own. The writing prompts in this section give you practice with this specialized form of journalism.

✦ REVIEWS

Prompts in this section let you be the reviewer. Reviewers, also called critics, share their opinion on recent books, movies, products, and more. Their work helps consumers make decisions about how to spend their time and money.

✦ SPORTS COVERAGE

Sports journalists pay attention to sports and games, competitions, athletes, and teams. They report on everything from school and local sports leagues to professional athletes and international sporting events, like the Olympics.

✦ FEATURES WRITING

Feature stories go beyond the headlines to take a closer look at ideas, people, and places. Some journalists focus on human interest stories, which often have an emotional angle. Others cover arts and culture. Feature stories include profiles of entertainers, activists, and elected leaders.

What will you do with all the work you put into this journal? Share it! Look for opportunities to publish your stories in a school newspaper. Pitch ideas to local papers. You may even decide to start your own publication or podcast to deliver news and information to your community. Your work matters!

What qualities do you think a person needs to be a good journalist? Why?

What sparks your curiosity? Make a list of things you might like to report on. Write down different ideas, events, or issues that interest you.

Arts and Culture. Business. Technology. Politics. Education. Sports. These are examples of topics—or beats—that journalists research and write about. What beat might you like to cover? Why?

The five Ws and one H are **WHO**, **WHAT**, **WHEN**, **WHERE**, **WHY**, and **HOW**. Find an article online or in your local newspaper. Can you identify the five Ws and one H within the article?

When you read an article, what details grab your attention? Journalists use sensory details to tell the story. Practice using your senses to take notes about your surroundings at this moment. What can you see, hear, smell, touch, and taste?

Can you set the scene? Use your powers of observation to describe an event or activity you remember going to. Try to make readers feel as if they were there!

Imagine you are writing about an upcoming school talent show. List three people, or sources, from your school who you could interview to learn about the event. Why is each source important?

Can you grab readers' attention? In journalism, the first sentence or paragraph of a story is called the "lede." A lede should make a reader want to keep reading the article. Write a lede for a story about a place or event you went to recently.

What's the kicker? That's what journalists call a story's final sentence or paragraph. Good kickers have impact! Read an article online or in a print newspaper or magazine. Write down its kicker here. What makes it stand out?

Think of a story you'd like to report. It can be about a person, place, or event. Find or take a photo to go with it, then write a photo caption. Describe what the photo shows, who is in it, and when it was taken.

If you were to start a magazine for kids, what topics would you cover? Why?

Who would be your dream person
to interview? List three well-known people
you would love to ask questions.
What makes each person noteworthy?

Pick one person from your list of dream people to interview. Who is it? List at least seven questions you would ask about their life and work.

Build your skills by interviewing a friend or family member. Write down their name and seven questions you will ask them. How will these questions help you to get to know them better?

The best quotes give readers a feel for a person's unique expertise, experience, and personality. What is your favorite quote from a book, TV show, or film? Copy it here. Why have you chosen it? Why is this a good quote?

Practice writing an email to a person you hope to interview. In your request, explain who you are and what you're writing about. Write a first draft of your email to them below.

Journalists are always coming up with story ideas. They pitch their ideas to editors. Imagine you are presenting to an editor. Think of a story you want to report. Then practice writing a pitch. Explain what the story is about, why readers will care, and why it needs to be told now.

News Coverage

How do you stay informed? Make a list of the newspapers, magazines, websites, and other sources that you and your family use to follow the news.

What recent news story makes you feel hopeful? Why? What are your favorite details from the story? If you can't think of one, explore news outlets for recent stories.

Journalists cover local, national, and global news. Which would you like to focus on? Why?

Professional journalists carry an official press badge. It's their pass to all sorts of exciting and world-changing events such as presidential inaugurations, important sporting events, and big awards shows. Where would you go with an official press badge? Why?

Do you have a nose for school news? Brainstorm ideas for topics you'd cover as a reporter for a school newspaper. What do students need to know? What might be of interest?

Check community calendars and bulletin boards for news about upcoming events. Jot down information about events that interest you. Which do you want to report on? Why?

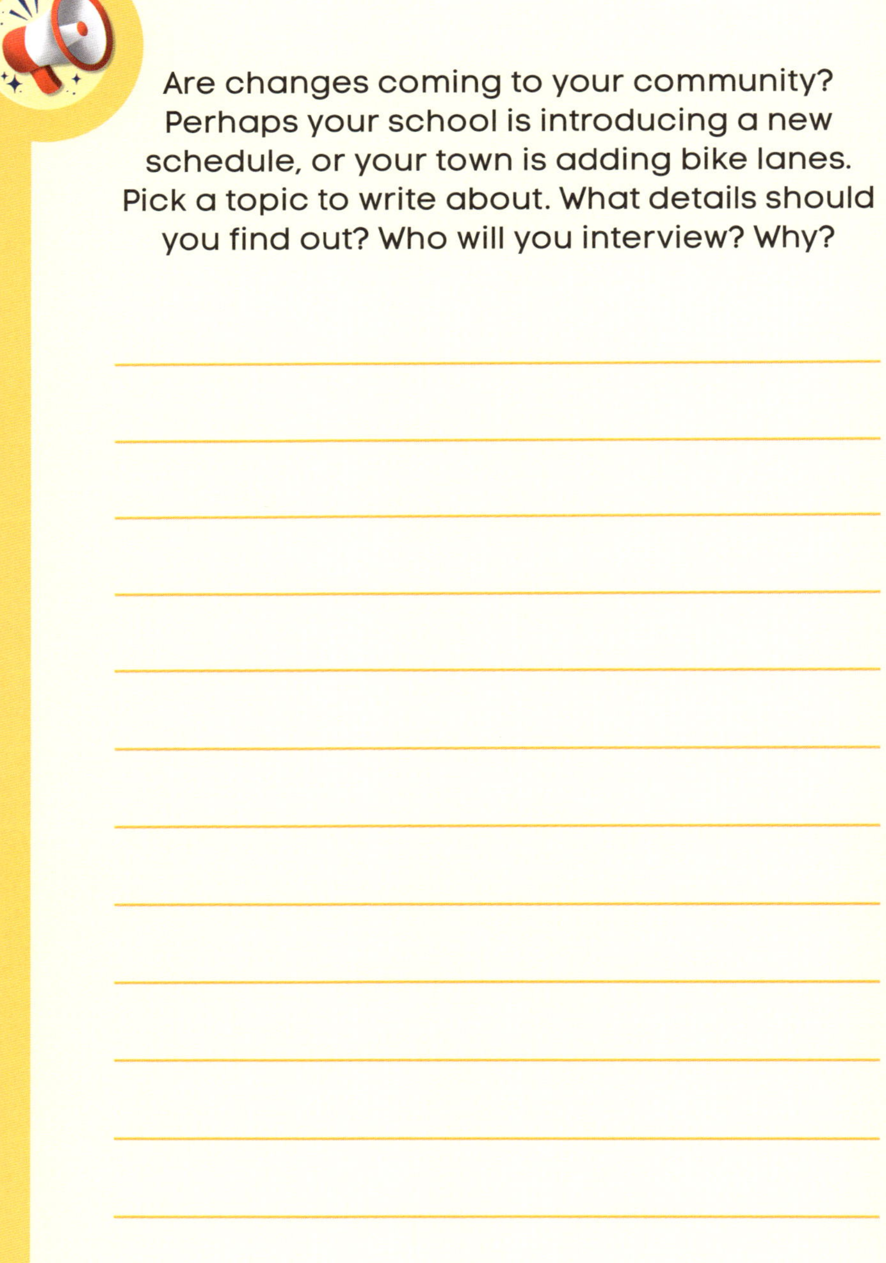

Are changes coming to your community? Perhaps your school is introducing a new schedule, or your town is adding bike lanes. Pick a topic to write about. What details should you find out? Who will you interview? Why?

Can you give a progress report? That's an update on a program or project that's being worked on. For example, how's a new program going at school? What work still needs to be done to complete a new building? List facts to include in your story.

What's the scoop with student government? Interview student council leaders! What goals are they working to achieve? What challenges do they face?

Have an adult you trust go with you to a city council meeting to report on local government. Who was there? What was discussed? What got people excited?

Business journalists write about the economy, money matters, companies, and stores. Pick a business or shop in your area to write about. Why is it newsworthy? What do people need to know?

Has a classmate or community member won an award or been recognized for an achievement? Write down seven questions you would ask them about the award and how they earned it. Then, interview them and record their responses.

Have you noticed a problem in your community? What is it? Who can you interview to learn about the problem and possible solutions?

Get the scoop on a class trip. Interview teachers and students to get different perspectives on the experience and what they learned from the field trip. Record their responses here.

What are students doing to help others? Write about a local community service project. What's the project? Who's involved? How is it helping people?

Report on current noteworthy weather conditions in your area. What are people doing to beat the heat? How are they coping with the cold? Interview several sources to get a variety of responses.

What's happening in animal news around the world? Have sea turtles hatched? Is there a new study about bears? Research an animal you care about. What would you cover in a news story about that animal? What facts will you focus on?

What's the latest in space? Rocket launches, eclipses, and scientific discoveries are examples of newsworthy events. Pick a recent development about space to report on. How will you explain the news in a way that readers can understand?

What's going on in other countries?
Read an international news story and then write about it. What is happening, and where? How are people there affected?

"Explainer" articles help readers understand complex topics in the news. Practice writing an explainer about a topic you know well, such as your favorite sport or a type of insect you've read a lot about. List questions someone might have about this subject. Then answer as clearly as you can.

What's new in your town? Fun examples include a playground, an ice-cream shop, or a community garden. Attend a grand opening event for a place in your community! Report what you learn. Remember to include answers to the five Ws and one H in your article (see page 9).

What's your opinion? Read a news article online or in your local paper. What do you think about what you read? How does it make you feel?

Can you write a letter to the editor?
Draft one in response to an article or
opinion column you've read.
What did you agree with in the article?
What did you disagree with?

Take a stand! Think about an issue affecting your school or community. What is it? How do you feel about it? Jot down your thoughts for an opinion article.

Who's the best candidate? Express your opinion on whom to vote for in a local, national, or school election. Why do you like the candidate? What qualifies them for the role?

What are your thoughts on a new project at school or in your community? What facts and details will you include in an article to support your opinion about the project?

How can your community be improved?
Pick one thing to focus on and explain
how you think you would make
your hometown better.

What would make your local playground more fun and inclusive for all kinds of kids? Survey kids of different ages to see what they think.

What matters to you? If you were old enough to vote, which issue would be most important to you when deciding whom to support in an election? Why?

What's the solution? Think about a problem you've read about in the news. In your opinion, what should be done to solve it?

Do "on the spot" interviews with students, teachers, and other people at your school to hear different points of view about a newsworthy topic or event. Come up with a simple question to ask everyone. Write down their responses.

A trend is something that's super popular for a short time. Do research for an opinion article about a new trend. What trend will you explore? Why? What facts and data will you include to support your opinion?

Should school uniforms be required? Do kids need smartphones? These are examples of debate questions. Make a list of other newsworthy questions you would like kids to weigh in on.

Pick a debate question from page 57. Write the question here. Research the issue. Then write an opinion article to express your point of view. Use facts and examples to support your position.

Write your selected debate question here again. Now argue the other side of the issue. Find facts and examples to support a different point of view.

Reviews help people decide what to read, what to watch, what to buy, and where to eat. Ask an adult about a time they made a decision based on a review. Was it helpful? Why?

Make a list of kid-friendly films you'd like to see. Pick one to review and then go watch it. Write down your thoughts as you watch. Did you enjoy the film? Why or why not?

Can you do a toy review?
What's your favorite? Why do you
recommend it to other kids?

Pick an album or a song to review.
On a scale of one to five stars, with one being the worst and five the best, what rating do you think it deserves? Why?

Go to a local museum. Choose an exhibition to visit and review. What's the exhibit? Why should others see it or skip it?

Pick a restaurant or other business to review. Which offerings did you and your family like best? Would you recommend it to others? Why?

At the end of every year, critics list their picks for the year's best books, movies, and other forms of entertainment. What would be on your list? Explain your choices.

What's a good present to give others? Write a gift guide to help readers pick presents for a specific group, such as moms, dads, teachers, or teens.

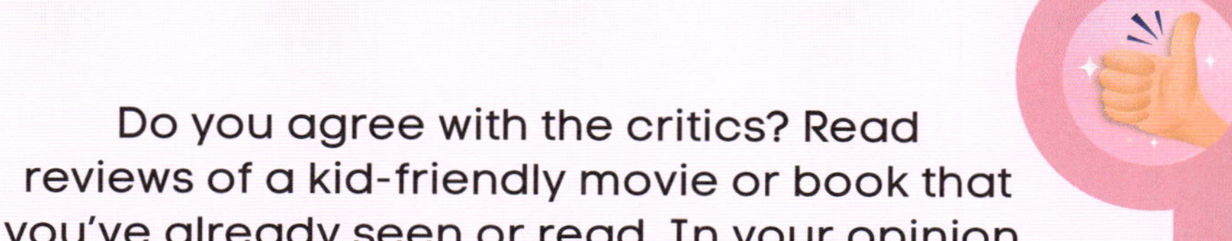

Do you agree with the critics? Read reviews of a kid-friendly movie or book that you've already seen or read. In your opinion, what do the critics get right or wrong?

What's a fun new book for kids? Ask a teacher or librarian for suggestions. Choose one to read and review. Explain the basic plot, then share your opinion. Whom would you recommend the book to? Why?

What sports story inspired you recently? Why?

Who's a top player? Choose a student athlete at your school to write about. What facts and statistics are important to include in your article? What should readers know about the player?

If you could interview a professional athlete, who would you choose? Why? What would you ask?

Pick a coach to profile. Who is it?
What accomplishments or character traits
make the coach newsworthy?

Which sport or activity is popular with kids in your community? What does a newcomer to the sport need to know about it? How can they get involved?

How are fans celebrating? Write about a victory celebration after a big game that you've personally witnessed or seen on TV. Use vivid details to capture the mood and remember to cover the five senses.

Can you give sports commentary? Watch a game to practice your live-reporting skills. What facts and opinions are important to share in a postgame wrap-up?

What makes a great sports photo?
Scan sports news to find a favorite image.
What does the photojournalist capture in
the image that words alone cannot?
Why do you personally like the photo?

Parkour. Ultimate Frisbee. Cheese rolling. These are examples of nontraditional sports. Brainstorm a list of others. Which sport do you feel deserves more coverage? How would you report on that sport?

How do fans show team spirit? Take notes on what you observe at a sporting event. Include examples such as their clothes, their signs, and their cheering.

Athletes aren't the only people who make sporting events come to life. What other people are important at a sporting event? How so? Who would be interesting to write about? Why?

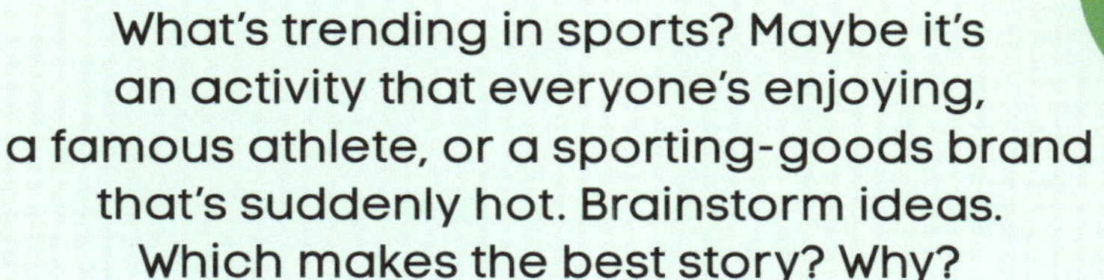

What's trending in sports? Maybe it's an activity that everyone's enjoying, a famous athlete, or a sporting-goods brand that's suddenly hot. Brainstorm ideas. Which makes the best story? Why?

What's your sports report? Write a news story about the results of a local sporting event, such as one that takes place at your school. Include highlights from the game. Interview a coach, players, and fans about the outcome.

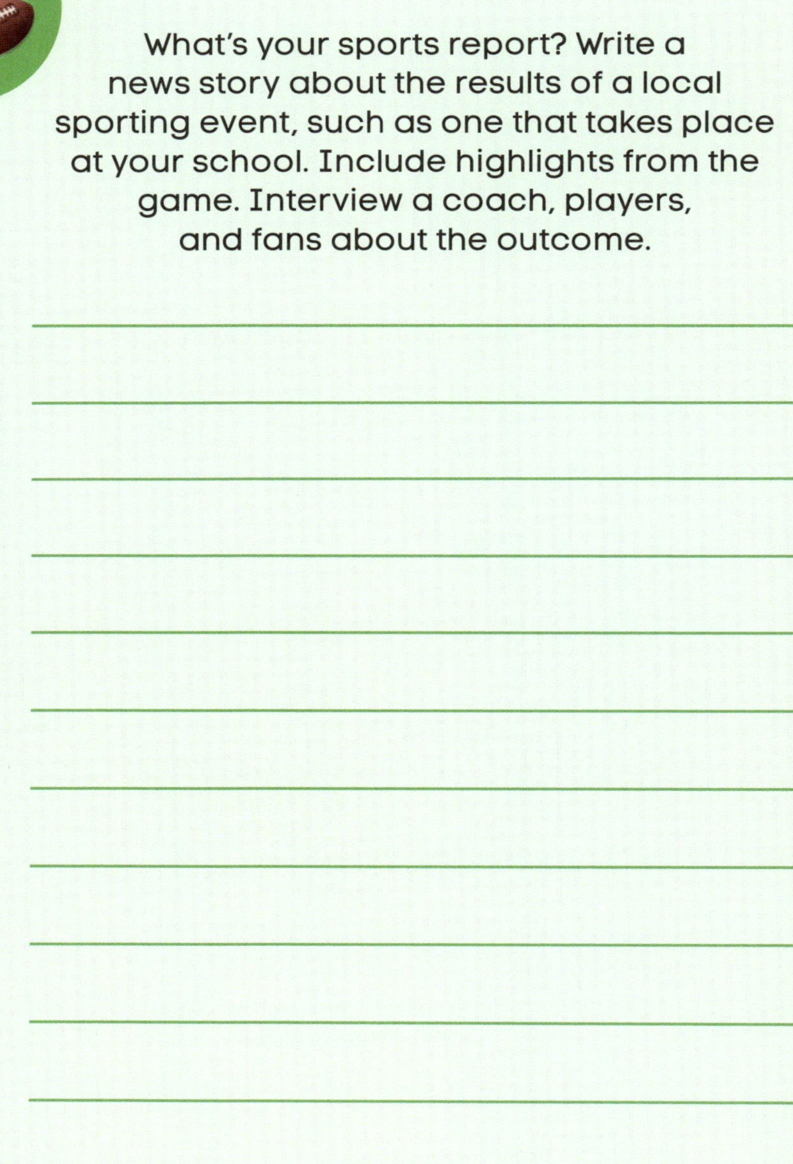

What makes a person worthy of being written about in a profile? What qualities do they have? What impact have they made? Make a list of people you consider noteworthy. Explain each.

Who's a star student? What makes the student newsworthy? What do others need to know about the student?

Who's making a difference in your community? What is this person doing to help others?

Ask permission to attend rehearsals for a school play or other performance. Take notes on what you observe for a story about what it takes to put on a show.

Spotlight a special teacher. Who will you pick? What will you ask in an interview? Ask questions that may reveal something fun, surprising, or unexpected and write down the teacher's responses below.

Do you know someone who cares deeply about the environment? Interview them about why they are so passionate about it and write down their responses. What are they doing to protect the environment?

Do you have a skill worth sharing? Do you work on this skill with anyone else? Interview a friend or classmate who has the same skill and ask them about how they practice it.

Is there a science, technology, or arts story people should know about? Are engineering advances happening in your community? Is math being used in interesting ways? What STEAM (science, technology, engineering, arts, or math) story interests you? How could you write an article about it?

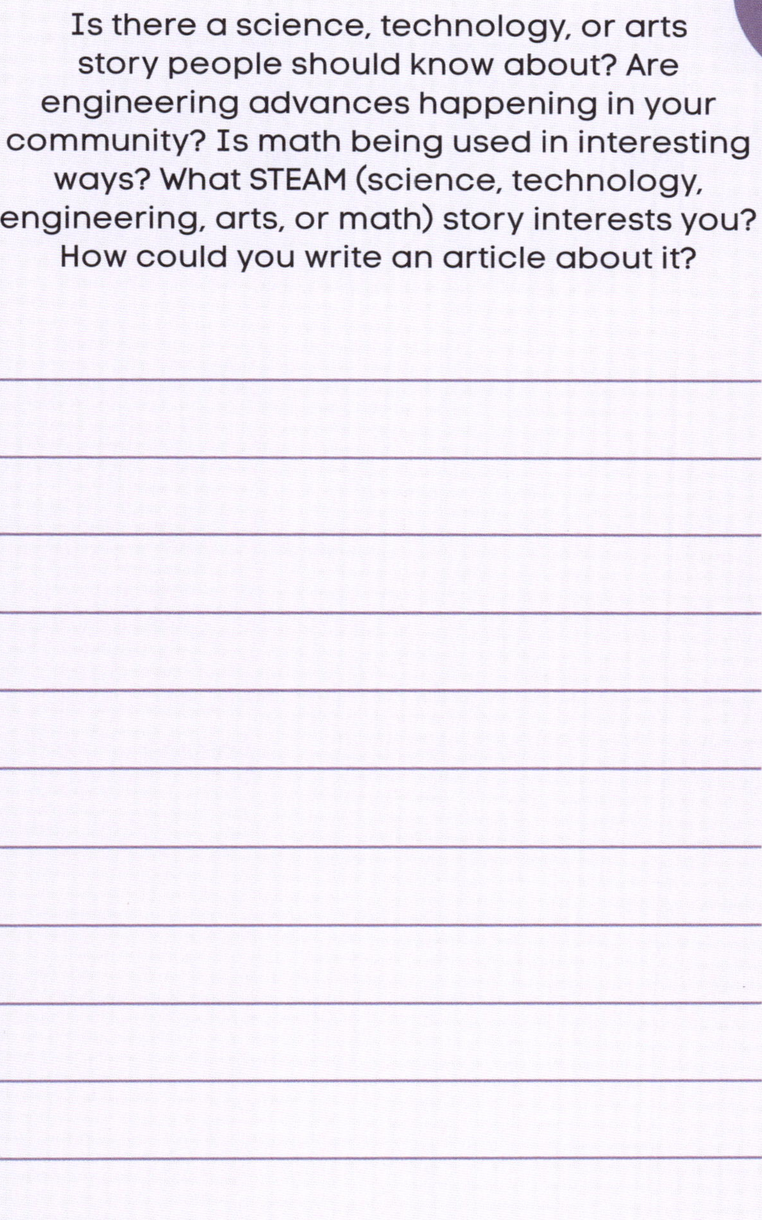

Write a travel story! What should a newcomer do on a visit to your town? What activities, attractions, foods, and cultural events can they experience?

A podcast is a series of audio episodes recorded by a host that cover a specific topic. If you made a podcast, what would it be about? Pick an interesting topic to report. Write a script to introduce the first episode.

Pick your favorite holiday. What's the history of the holiday? What do you already know about it? What questions will you explore in your article?

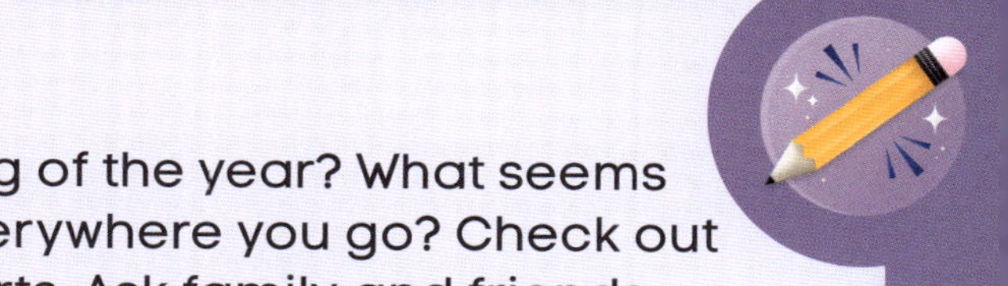

What's the song of the year? What seems to be playing everywhere you go? Check out the music charts. Ask family and friends. What makes the song so popular, and what are some records that it has broken or set?

What's the history of your school?
Find out all you can and write a story on it!
Who is it named after? When did it open?
How has it changed over time?

Historical plaques and markers tell us about our communities. Find one that interests you. What details would you include in a story? What research and reporting will you do to learn more?

What is your town's favorite treat? What makes the food "famous" in your community? Write a story about how it came to be.

How do you like to learn? What are your teachers doing to make learning fun and engage students in new and different ways? Write a story about your favorite way to learn and how your teacher makes it happen.

Has a new mural, sculpture, or other work of public art recently been added to your community? Write about it! What would you like to know about the artist and the artwork?

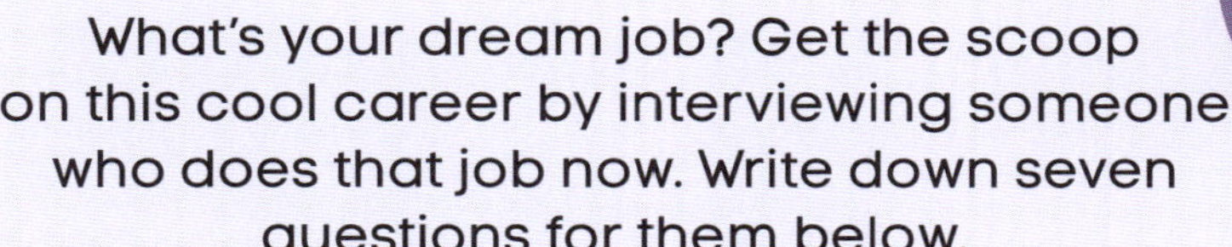

What's your dream job? Get the scoop on this cool career by interviewing someone who does that job now. Write down seven questions for them below.

What's trending with people your age?
Is it a fun fashion? A must-try treat?
A popular toy? Pick one to research and
write about. Why did you choose it?

What new technology is everyone talking about? How is it being used? What are the effects, both positive and negative, of this technology? Write what you learn below.

Is there an issue at your school or in your community that doesn't get enough attention? How would you write a story about it?

How has your community changed for the better? Interview people who have lived in the area for a long time. What positive changes have they observed?

Many families mark holidays with special traditions. What's yours? How and when did it start? What makes it meaningful?

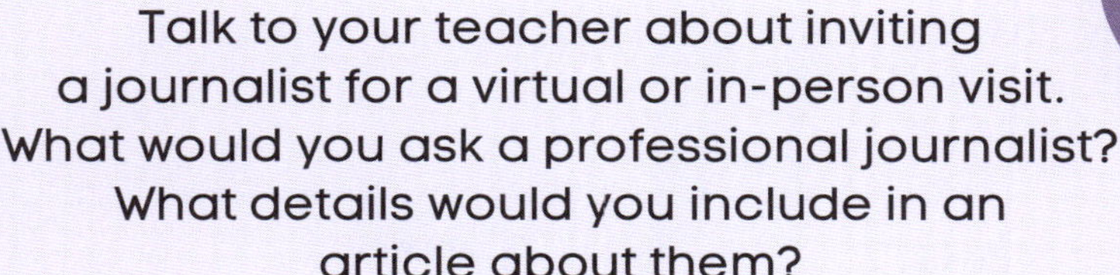

Talk to your teacher about inviting a journalist for a virtual or in-person visit. What would you ask a professional journalist? What details would you include in an article about them?

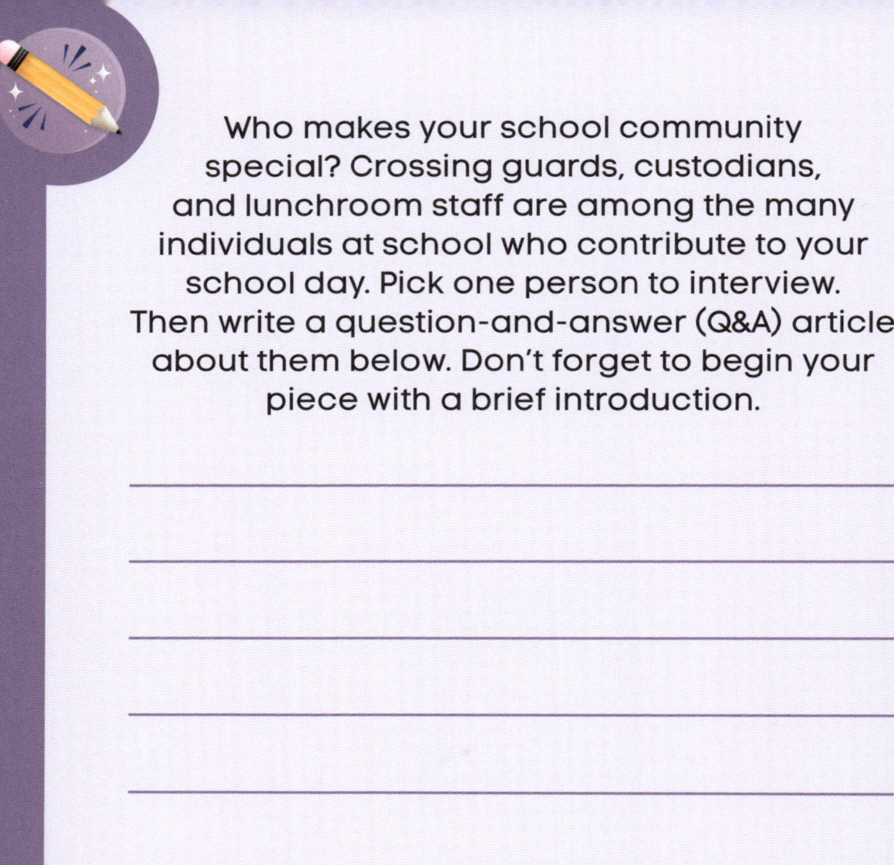

Who makes your school community special? Crossing guards, custodians, and lunchroom staff are among the many individuals at school who contribute to your school day. Pick one person to interview. Then write a question-and-answer (Q&A) article about them below. Don't forget to begin your piece with a brief introduction.

Also Available

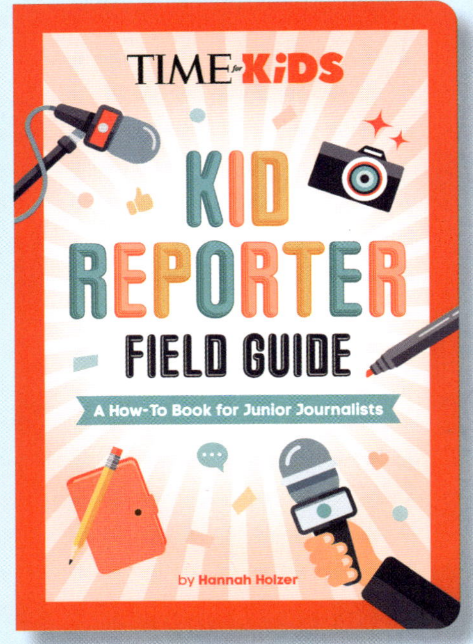